Funny Puppies

J. C. Suarès and Jana Martin

Welcome

New York

Published in 1999 by Welcome Enterprises, Inc.

588 Broadway, New York, NY 10012

(212) 343-9430 Fax (212) 343-9434

Creative Director: J. C. Suarès

Editor: Jana Martin

Designer: Hasmig M. Kacherian

Library of Congress Card Catalogue Number: 99-62196

Printed and bound in Singapore

10   9   8   7   6   5   4   3   2   1

frontispiece:
KARL WEATHERLY
St. Bernard Pup on a Hot Day
Chapel Hill, North Carolina, 1973

title page:
BERNARD HOFFMAN
Christina and Her Weimaraner
Ridgefield, Connecticut, 1950

right:
ROBIN SCHWARTZ
Juliet Scott, French Bull Dog, at Three Months
Brooklyn, New York, 1996

INTRODUCTION

A friend in the Marine Corps stopped by one night with a Dalmatian puppy. He said he'd rescued the dog from some unpleasant situation (which he wouldn't elaborate on) and, since he couldn't take care of it himself, living on a military post and all that, he felt I should.

The first day, while I was out, the puppy ate a pair of brown loafers, a leather-bound collection of Shakespeare sonnets, my best belt, and three fingers off the left hand of my favorite pair of gloves. I'd been gone for five hours. Clearly this guy didn't like to be left alone.

I tried a two-pronged approach over the next few days. If this hyper little puppy didn't get constant attention, he'd go after the nearest leather object. So I spent as much time as possible with him. And I learned to hide things.

He still kept finding stuff to chew on. So when I had to drive somewhere, I took him with me. While I was at the wheel of my carefully restored vintage car, concentrating on the road, he silently destroyed the armrest in the back seat. Then I brought him to my studio. While I was drawing, he devoured my watercolors. I turned around to find a dog that looked like he'd been practicing clown make-up. His face was streaked in Prussian blue, cadmium red, and chromium green.

I felt terribly inadequate. If he had to destroy things even in my company, then obviously I was doing something wrong. I'll get him some toys, I thought. I rushed out and bought a dozen, in rawhide. Back home I humbly presented them, placing them on the floor. Surrounded by these peace offerings he looked up at me, expressionless.

I left him alone. He left the toys alone. The next day he overturned the garbage and feasted on half a dozen babas au rhum, those French pastries soaked in liqueur. I found him on the kitchen floor, sleeping off his drunken binge, and smelling like an old barfly. He was covered in the debris that had given him so much pleasure: old lettuce, burnt toast, and pastry crumbs.

But I couldn't stay mad. After all, he was just a puppy. Maybe soon he'd realize the toys were there for him, and would lose interest in my shoes. He might even grow up to be another Lassie.

I came home optimistic the next day. I walked in to discover he hadn't touched the toys. He hadn't found any stray shoes either. Instead, he'd eaten my passport. Multicolored pulp was all that was left.

This was the last straw.

There was, of course, one redeeming aspect to the episode. I got to walk into the passport office and utter that famous excuse to the ink-stained clerk. "My dog ate it," I told him, and received a priceless look of disdain.

A week later, when a repairman working on the house confessed he was crazy about my Dalmatian, I knew exactly what to do. "Take him," I said.

From what I understand, the dog never destroyed anything else. But he still managed to cloak himself in notoriety. When the repairman and his girlfriend split up, she dognapped the puppy. The last time I saw the repairman he looked like hell, obsessed with getting back his dog. He had a paper for me to sign, stating that the dog had been a present to him and him alone. "I wouldn't call it a present," I started to say, then stopped myself. I found a pen, signed my name, and wished him the best of luck.

—*J.C. Suarès*

The great pleasure of a dog is that you

may make a fool of yourself with him

and not only will he not scold you, but

he will make a fool of himself too.

SAMUEL BUTLER, 1912

NINA LEEN
A Brand New Shetland Sheepdog
U.S., 1950

A Big Surprise

At the animal shelter my son picked out this tiny little puppy that squeaked. I thought, this dog will be easy. He'll grow up to be the size of a Cocker Spaniel at the most. Well, now he weighs a hundred pounds and eats nine times a day. And he's only ten months old.

ANNE ZHAO

ARCHITECT

LOS ANGELES

PHOTOGRAPHER UNKNOWN
When Great Hunters Meet
London, England, 1970

JOHN DRYSDALE
Monkey Mothercare for a Jack Russell Terrier
Coventry, England, 1988

WALTER CHANDOHA
In the Doghouse
Long Island, New York, 1961

I am called a dog because I fawn

on those who give me anything,

I yelp at those who refuse, and I

set my teeth on rascals.

DIOGENES THE CYNIC, 4TH CENTURY BC

ROBIN SCHWARTZ
Billy, Jack Russell Terrier, at Five Months
Montclair, New Jersey, 1995

Definition

They are I think called Chihuahuas because they chew on everything including my toys.

JESSIE ROSE

KINDERGARTNER

SYRACUSE

PAUL VAN DRIEL/ERIK ALBLAS
Two Together: Chihuahua Puppies
Amsterdam, 1993

overleaf:
ALLAN AND SANDY CAREY
Bloodhound Mother and Child
Montana, 1994

ROBIN SCHWARTZ
Copper
Hoboken, New Jersey, 1995

Please Don't Go

Madge is a Rotteweiler, big as a pony now and queen of the house. But even as a puppy she threw her weight around. She somehow knew if I was headed out the door without her. So she'd go sit on my shoes.

STEVE SCHWARTZ

ARTIST

BROOKLYN

PAUL VAN DRIEL/ERIK ALBLAS
Still Life with Sneaker and Chihuahua
Dordrecht, Holland, 1993

24

Natural Selection

My job at the pet food company involved testing puppy food. The procedure wasn't very scientific: it was based purely on pup appeal. I'd release a puppy into a room with two separate flavor prototypes and see which one he went for. One beagle puppy made his choice very clear. First he gobbled up the entire contents of bowl #1. Then he toddled over to bowl #2 and peed in it.

LINDA THOMAS

FORMER PET FOOD TESTER

CHICAGO

CLARENCE SINCLAIR BULL
Maureen O'Sullivan and Junior, Her Toy Fox Terrier Puppy
Hollywood, California, 1933

YOICHI R. OKAMOTO
A Basket Full of Beagles
The White House, Washington, D.C., 1966

MIKE SARGENT
President George Bush and Millie, English
Springer Spaniel, with Her
Puppies on the South Lawn
The White House, Washington, D.C., 1989

PRISCILLA RATTAZZI
Two Honeys on the Wagon (Luna and Sasha)
East Hampton, New York, 1997

right:
KARL BADEN
Untitled
Boston, Massachusets, 1987

Just a Phase

Whitey, our three-month-old Neopolitan Mastiff, is really dark gray. His bones are made of rubber and he never walks, he galumphs. When his feet give out—about every other minute—he rolls the rest of the way. Last week he dive-bombed a pile of cherry jello my daughter accidentally dropped on the kitchen floor. Then he ambushed a pile of clean laundry. My daughter, who's six, will not let us scold him. She says this is Whitey's preschool phase, when kids are supposed to make a mess.

JACK RANGLE

MUSIC PRODUCER

SACRAMENTO

STEPHANIE RAUSSER
Eva, Labrador Puppy
Berkeley, California, 1990

Guilty

One rainy night we found a tiny stray puppy on the street and brought her home. To show her gratitude she chased our cats into the bathroom, pulled the covers off our bed, shat on the oriental rug, and raided the pantry. She ate an entire box of Meow Mix, including the cardboard. We caught her red-handed, but I suspect her guilty look was just an act.

SARA DAWSON LEVIN

CHEF

SEATTLE

SANTA CLARA POLICE DEPARTMENT
Dog-Tagged
Santa Clara, California, 1988

CITY OF SANTA CLARA
POLICE DEPARTMENT

5   0 7 0 8 '88

ROBIN SCHWARTZ
Helen, Shar Pei, at Twelve Weeks
Staten Island, New York, 1997

overleaf:
RALPH CRANE
A Christmas Airedale for Raymond and Susie
Northridge, California, 1971

A Sneaky Sweetie

When I was young we had a Samoyed, Sobaka (dog in Russian). He was a bitey, domineering dog who had to be the boss, though there was much love between us. In the winter we'd hitch him up to a sled—that was his proudest moment. A few years later we got another Samoyed to keep him company. She was a real sweetheart named Zöe. But she was also a master thief. Anything big old Sobaka had—a ball, a bone, a stick, a treat, even a smelly old sock—she'd take. She'd wait patiently nearby until he was distracted, then sneak up right under his nose to nab the prize and romp away. Sobaka never knew what happened.

EVE MINKOFF

EDITOR

MASSACHUSETTS

KENT AND DONNA DANNEN
Samoyed "Chinook" CD, WS, and Her Pup
Estes Park, Colorado, 1986

GREGORY WAKABAYASHI
Yogi and Bowl
New York City, 1999

right:
WALTER CHANDOHA
Sweetie with Bottle
Annadale, New Jersey, 1970

Of the pup: discourage biting, for that will decrease his civility, but encourage his antics, for that will increase his intelligence. You may let him roam, but insist he mind your borders. For like any youth, a pup will be careless and disloyal; prone to wandering and picking up fleas.

GENTLEMAN'S HANDBOOK, 19TH CENTURY

NINA LEEN
Tank, Three-Month-Old Yorkshire Terrier Puppy
Westport, Connecticut, 1964

ROBIN SCHWARTZ
Nell, English Bull Dog Puppy, at Thirteen Weeks
Jersey City, New Jersey, 1995

right:
Petie, Rescued Chihuahua Mix
Jersey City, New Jersey 1995

overleaf, left, and right:
Mattie, Jack Russell Puppy, at Five Months
New York City, 1995

Tia, Chihuahua, at Three Months
Hudson, New Hampshire, 1998

left:

MASATOSHI MAKINO
Golden Retriever Puppy
Okinawa, Japan, 1996

TOMONORI TANIGUCHI
What a Life
Gunma Prefecture, Japan, 1994

JOHN DRYSDALE
My Powerful Friend
Banbury, England, 1989

WALTER CHANDOHA
Weimaraners on the Loose
Long Island, New York, 1971

PHOTOGRAPHER UNKNOWN
The Gargoyles Stand Guard
U.S., c. 1970

overleaf, left:
ROBIN SCHWARTZ
Ethan and Rue, Seven-Week-Old Whippet Puppies
Philadelphia, Pennsylvania, 1996

overleaf, right:
DONNA RUSKIN
Maxi and Sammy Looking Sheepish
New York City, 1998

pp. 62–63, and 64–65:
ROBIN SCHWARTZ
The Diablesse Whippets: Vello, Aprila, Guy,
Liam, Truly, and Wilham
Morristown, New Jersey, 1995

The Uschi Von Jens English Bull Dogs: Bart, Homer,
Winston, Bella, Maggie, and Sarah
Tenafly, New Jersey, 1996

A Puppy's Point of View

Our dog Pepper had six puppies. They're little fluff balls. They don't know anything when they're born. They think Pepper will leave them alone and never feed them unless they follow her everywhere and cry. They think the cat is a monster and that my hand is a chew toy, and that the backyard is a giant forest and they are the great hunters. If I lie down on the floor, they come and climb all over me. Then, they think I'm a mountain.

DAN PATTERSALL

KINDERGARTNER

PITTSBURGH

MASATOSHI MAKINO
Puppy Pals
Okinawa, Japan, 1996

Few quadrupeds are less

delicate in their food.

OLIVER GOLDSMITH, 1774

YLLA
Collie Puppy and Siamese Kitten in My Studio
New York City, 1947

The Young Connoisseur

Fidel, our Shepherd puppy, finds peanut butter irresistible. Also butter, chocolate milk, any kind of ice cream, and spaghetti with olive oil. I think the rule is that if it's all over Fidel's fur, it tastes even better. His breeder promises me he'll get more dignified with age. And I always say, Can I get a second opinion on that?

JOE McBRIDE

WRITER

BOSTON

NANCY LEVINE
Four-Month-Old Maxie and Her Big Sister Lulu,
Miniature Australian Shepherds
New York City, 1995

overleaf:
ROBIN SCHWARTZ
Bella Rose, Beagle Puppy, at Eleven Weeks
Jersey City, New Jersey, 1995

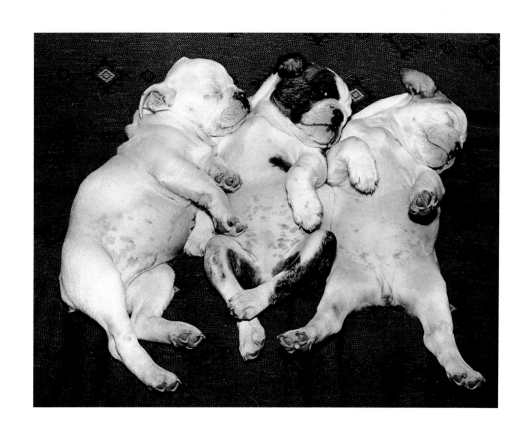

ROBIN SCHWARTZ
Egypt, Butchie, and Dotty Kuharic, English Bull Dogs
New York City, 1996

RYOHEI AKIMOTO
My Friend's New Puppies Look Around
Japan, 1986

preceding pages:

MAGNUS WALLER

Finally, They Sleep

Stockholm, Sweden, 1975

right:

PHOTOGRAPHER UNKNOWN

Alfie Gets a Free Ride

New York City, 1970